# YOUR KNOWLEDGE HAS VALUE

Samir Huseynov

# One more efficiency test for market economy-Return to Schooling

**Does market economy reward education more than communism?**

GRIN Verlag

**Bibliografische Information der Deutschen Nationalbibliothek:**

Die Deutsche Bibliothek verzeichnet diese Publikation in der Deutschen National-
bibliografie; detaillierte bibliografische Daten sind im Internet über http://dnb.d-
nb.de/ abrufbar.

**Imprint:**

Copyright © 2009 GRIN Verlag GmbH
Druck und Bindung: Books on Demand GmbH, Norderstedt Germany
ISBN: 978-3-656-12657-7

**This book at GRIN:**

http://www.grin.com/en/e-book/188822/one-more-efficiency-test-for-market-eco-
nomy-return-to-schooling

**One more efficiency test for market economy-Return to Schooling:**

**Does market economy reward education more than communism?**

**By Samir Huseynov**

**Literature Review and Motivation**

This paper aims to analyze the change in return to schooling in Hungary, via comparing communism and market economy periods. As the philosophy of each system is very different, it causes differences in treatment of factors of production as well. While getting familiar with main literature of this topic, it turns out that there is not consensus about the main driving philosophy of communism in terms of organizing production. There are some contradictory assumptions on rewarding factors of production, especially personal characteristics under planned economy. According to one them, because of egalitarian approach towards workers, wage profiles were compressed and planners set wages on the base of industry and work profile under communism (Campos and Joliffe, (2003)). So personal characteristics like education were not evaluated and that is why after transition to market economy in ex-communist countries return to education should increase. But other assumption states that planners were well informed about the importance of personal traits in productivity and they kept total wage fund for a firm fixed, while allowing managers to distribute available money within firm according to performance and personal properties (Robert Chase, (1998)). Wage grid was one of the ways, to evaluate education. So, this assumption concludes that, after transition education didn't yield more return than it was previously. But, as Bergson (1944) argued, managers had to follow ceilings and floors, so under planned economy return to education was lower than it should be and after transition return should increase. Also, according to Schultz(1975) a more educated person is more successful in adjustment to disequilibrium, which means in new system, more educated people would achieve better job and would get more for their education, than it was in previous system. In summary of above

discussion, we can conclude that, although some assumptions claim possible decrease in return to schooling in former communist countries after transition to market economy, mainstream literature support first stated approach –increase in return to education in market economy. So, this paper sheds light to theoretical discussions via quantitative analysis and aims to find some empirical evidences. Beyond this, my paper can give some insights about efficiency of planned economy and market economy and can serve as a new milestone in long lasting debate between supporters of two systems. As you know, in last century, humanity experienced rivalry of market economy and communism. Superiority of each system was claimed by their proponents throughout sharp debates, which lasted approximately more than a century. After the collapse of SSSR and its communist block, post communist countries transformed their economic systems to market economy. In today's world there are still several countries with planned economy, like China with huge economic growth. So, the humanity still has alternative choice in terms of economic systems and "Which one is better? " is still open question, at least for modern communist economists after the experience of recent economic crises. So, I think my paper can be "fresh" voice in this debate as well.

The experiences of ex-communist but new market economies of Eastern Europe are good natural experiment. With pure communist history these countries achieved more sophisticated market economy institutions than former SSSR countries. Among post communist block countries, Hungary is more appropriate for this study, as Hungary showed the highest score in the EBRD index of market-supporting institutions for 2001 (EBRD, 2002, p. 9). Taking these facts into the consideration in this paper, I focus on Hungary and aim to find some empirical evidences from Hungary's experience.

## Data

The individual level data was retrieved from Hungarian Wage survey and covers the year 1986, which was communist era and the year 2004 which was the beginning of EU

membership in Hungary. Unfortunately it is not panel data, but by using some econometric tools we can get proper results from pooled-cross sectional data as well. Data includes rw (real wage), exp (experience), edu (years of education), ind (industry dummy), reg (region dummy). More precisely: rw is real monthly earnings (adjusted to 2005 price level) and includes base salary and other pecuniary items of worker compensation (like regular bonuses, premia, overtime pay and etc.). Edu is years of education. In retrieved data education of individuals was described by levels of educational system in 5 categories: 1-less than elementary, 2-elementary, 3-vocational, 4-high school, 5-university or college. In order to make my empirical model to work I replaced them with average years of schooling. Here I used the information provided by Ministry of Hungarian Education and Culture (http://www.okm.gov.hu/letolt/english/education_in_hungary_080805.pdf) and on the base of my own calculation I replaced "less than elementary" with 5 years, "elementary" with 8 years, -"vocational" with 11 years, "high school" with 12 years, "university or college" with 16 years. Exp is potential years of experience (calculated by the source). Ind includes industry dummies (only one and two digits industry codes according to ISIC): agriculture, mining and light industry (production of dressing, leather etc, this term with the term heavy industry is still widely used by ex-Communist countries), heavy industry (production of chemicals, metal products etc.), utilities, service, transport, business, education, other services (like Sewage and refuse disposal, sanitation and similar activities and etc.). Here for the sake of simplicity I codified two digits industry classifications under same category (e.g. from 20 to 37 were described with heavy industry). Reg dummies include: 1 - Central Hungary, 2 - Central Transdanubia, 3 - Western Transdanubia, 4 - Southern Transdanubia, 5 - Northern Hungary, 6 - Northern Great Plain, 7 - Southern Great Plain.

**Empirical framework**

To analyze change in return to schooling I primarily use (OLS) earnings equations based on Mincer(1974)- regressing log real wage log(rw) on years of schooling(edu), years of potential experience(exp) and experience squared($\exp 2$ )

$$\log(rw) = b_0 + b_1 edu + b_2 \exp + b_3 \exp 2$$

Then, I added industry and region dummies. Because of self-selection, people with high ability may get more education and may tend to work in industries like banking, where mostly more educated people are concentrated and return is higher then other industries (Juhn, Murphy and Pierce (1993)). So choice of industry to work may be endogenous and that is why I controlled industry by ind dummies. Similar arguments can be used for reg dummy, as choice of place might be endogenous. Usually, people try to live in cities, especially in capital, where return to education is higher, as education intensive industries are located (mostly) in cities. So, I controlled region effect by reg dummies as well. (see Robert Chase (1998) for similar framework). Usually, self selection problem can be removed with maximum likelihood – generalized Tobit approach, but it is the beyond of my paper's scope. In labor economics literature it is approximately consensus that earning determinants of males and females are different, that is why I split wage data for males and females and regressions were done for each of them separately. The following first equation is designed to capture return to schooling for males in 1986, the second for males 2004, the third for females 1986, the fourth for females 2004. X is a vector of all above indicated variables and B is vector of coefficients of those variables.

$$\log(rw_{m86}) = \alpha_{m86} + BX_{m86} + \varepsilon$$

$$\log(rw_{m04}) = \alpha_{m04} + BX_{m04} + \varepsilon$$

$$\log(rw_{f86}) = \alpha_{f86} + BX_{f86} + \varepsilon$$

$$\log(rw_{f04}) = \alpha_{f04} + BX_{f04} + \varepsilon$$

## Results

By processing Mincer(1974), I got results, which are described in Table1. For male respondents return to education rose from 0.05 to 0.14, for females from 0.04 to 0.14. It means one more year of schooling increased returns 5% for males and 4% for females under planned economy, but in market economy it was 14% for both genders. So we observe significant increase to return to schooling after transition to market economy. But for potential experience, we observe decline from 0.05 to 0.02 for males and from 0.04 to 0.03 for females. It shows that, experience gained in communism became obsolete or was not as useful as it was under planned economy after transition, mostly because of huge change in technology and over all organization of economy. In market economy post production process, like marketing, sale, competition strategy are very important, which were ignored in communism.

**Table1** *(t-statistics are in parentheses, full regression tables are available upon request)*

*Regressions were done by Eviews 6*

Table1

| Dependent variable: log(real wage) | Male Respondents 1986 | 2004 | Female Respondents 1986 | 2004 |
|---|---|---|---|---|
| Intercept | 10.63 | 9.69 | 10.47 | 9.58 |
| | (-671.66) | (190.64) | (761.35) | (197.91) |
| Years of Education | 0.05 | 0.14 | 0.04 | 0.14 |
| | (-49.46) | (42.74) | (44.36) | (42.17) |
| Experience(potential) | 0.05 | 0.02 | 0.04 | 0.03 |
| | (-54.52) | (7.5) | (47.8) | (12.87) |
| Experience(potential) squared | -0.0001 | -0.0002 | -0.0007 | -0.0004 |
| | (-48.86) | (-5.8) | (-39.48) | (-9.73) |
| Number of respondents | 28116 | 6154 | 25633 | 5631 |
| R-squared | 0.159 | 0.231 | 0.145 | 0.252 |

As discussed above, then I extended estimation by adding region and industry dummies. From Table 2, it is obvious that in first three columns R-squared increased (e.g. for male respondents in 1986, R-squared increased from 0.159 to 0.187), which means by adding new

**Table2** *(t-statistics are in parentheses, full regression tables are available upon request)*

*Regressions were done by Eviews 6. In table agriculture, light industry, mining and Central*

| Dependent variable: log(real wage) | Male 1986 | Respondents 2004 | Female 1986 | Respondents 2004 |
|---|---|---|---|---|
| Intercept | 10.77 | 9.90 | 10.58 | 9.83 |
| | (517.97) | (182.13) | (728.87) | (198.27) |
| Years of Education | 0.05 | 0.13 | 0.04 | 0.12 |
| | (38.52) | (40.25) | (42.49) | (37.70) |
| Experience(potential) | 0.05 | 0.02 | 0.04 | 0.03 |
| | (55.98) | (7.63) | (48.72) | (13.90) |
| Experience(potential) squared | -0.0009 | -0.0003 | -0.0007 | -0.0004 |
| | (-47.27) | (-6.02) | (-40.08) | (-11.14) |
| Transdanubia | -0.10 | -0.11 | NA | -0.16 |
| | (-6.40) | (0.03) | NA | (-6.91) |
| Western Transdanubia | -0.13 | -0.07 | -0.15 | -0.16 |
| | (-9.32) | (-2.79) | (-18.61) | (-7.02) |
| Southern Transdanubia | -0.13 | -0.07 | -0.15 | -0.21 |
| | (-8.93) | (-8.23) | (-19.28) | (-8.51) |
| Northern Hungary | -0.17 | -0.19 | -0.20 | -0.27 |
| | (-11.19) | (-6.96) | (-22.30) | (-11.89) |
| Northern Great Plain | -0.18 | -0.21 | -0.19 | -0.26 |
| | (-14.86) | (0.02) | (-26.38) | (-12.13) |
| Southern Great Plain | -0.15 | -0.18 | -0.14 | -0.24 |
| | (-12.83) | (-7.82) | (-20.24) | (-11.98) |
| Heavy industry | -0.009 | 0.11 | 0.06 | 0.16 |
| | (-0.68) | (4.56) | (5.30) | (3.52) |
| Utilities | 0.003 | 0.008 | 0.01 | 0.08 |
| | (0.17) | (0.25) | (6.07) | (2.09) |
| Service | -0.10 | -0.12 | 0.006 | -0.04 |
| | (-10.33) | (-4.59) | (1.10) | (-1.90) |
| Transport | 0.04 | 0.20 | 0.26 | 0.38 |
| | (1.56) | (6.83) | (18.86) | (18.63) |
| Business | -0.03 | -0.04 | 0.07 | 0.04 |
| | (-2.00) | (-1.38) | (6.38) | (1.34) |
| Education | -0.0003 | -0.12 | NA | -0.13 |
| | (-0.008) | (-1.42) | NA | (-2.42) |
| Other services | -0.0004 | -0.01 | 0.08 | 0.04 |
| | (-0.008) | (-0.27) | (3.06) | (0.86) |
| Number of Respondents | 28116 | 6154 | 25633 | 5631 |
| R-squared | 0.187 | 0.274 | 0.210 | 0.361 |

*Hungary were excluded.*

variables I got the chance of capturing more variation in data. But, we again have similar results for our target variable and it means our first estimation was successful in disclosing relationships between years to schooling and earnings. In second estimation for male respondents return to schooling rose from 0.05 to 0.13 and for females from 0.04 to 0.12. And again we see decrease in the coefficients of potential experience for males from 0.05 to 0.02 and for females from 0.04 to 0.03.

## Conclusion

The main quantitative outcome of my paper is that, after transition to market economy return to schooling were increased both for men and women. More exactly for males it went from 5% to 13% and for females from 4% to 12%. So, does it mean that market economy rewards education more than communism? Although my results leads to answering "YES", but I should be careful. Because there are some caveats in my empirical model. First, due to measurement error in data, self selection bias (which can be ruled out by generalized Tobit approach) my results are biased. And also I did not control ability in my estimation which might cause serious bias in estimation. But after all, I think my results can give some intuition regarding efficiency in two systems and be "fresh" quantitative milestone in above mentioned debate.

## References

Campos, N., Jolliffe, D., 2002. After, Before And During: Returns to Education in the Hungarian Transition. William Davidson Institute Working Paper 475.


Mincer, J. and Polachek, S. (1974), 'Family Investments in Human Capital: Earnings of Women', Journal of Political Economy, 82(2, part 2): S76–S108.

Robert Chase, (Apr 1998) Markets for Communist Human Capital: Returns to eEducation and experience in the Czech republic and Slovakia, pp 401-423,Cornell University Press,